36 Views of Fuji

ALSO BY KENTON WING ROBINSON

The Water Sonnets
Ao (as Suzume Shi)

36 Views of Fuji

Poems by

Kenton Wing Robinson

Antrim House
Bloomfield, Connecticut

Copyright © 2022 by Kenton Wing Robinson

Except for short selections reprinted for purposes of
book review, all reproduction rights are reserved.
Requests for permission to replicate should
be addressed to the publisher.

Library of Congress Control Number: 9781943826995

ISBN: 978-1-943826-99-5

First Edition, 2022

Printed & bound by Ingram Content Group

Book design by Rennie McQuilkin

Front cover photograph by Christofer Tan on Unsplash

Antrim House
860.519.1804
antrimhousebooks@gmail.com
www.antrimhousebooks.com
400 Seabury Dr., Bloomfield, CT 06002

For Lorikay, my sun & wind & rain

"*Write?*" *you said.*
"*Two lines.*
"*You only need to write two lines.*"

Acknowledgments

Grateful acknowledgment to the editors of the following publications in which certain poems in this volume first appeared, some in earlier versions:

Karamu, Nisqually Delta, Coal Hill Review, Lilliput Review, Red Owl, Literary Mama and *The Indented Pillow*

My thanks to Rennie McQuilkin, editor and publisher of Antrim House, who transforms my scrawl into books of beauty. And to Michael W. Howard, my closest reader and, *pace* Aristotle, second self.

36 Views of Fuji: Letters to My Muse

Just as the artist Hokusai created 36 views of Mount Fuji and made 102 black and white woodblock prints of same, so each month for 27 years, I wrote a letter to my muse, until I had written nine books of 36 poems each.

That, at least, is the conceit of this collection. In fact, the bones of some of these poems are more than 50 years old. And the "you" addressed in any particular poem may be my muse or another.

Each poem is in a form of my invention: nine lines in three stanzas, with no stanza longer than 17 syllables. Sometimes stanzas will be broken up, but no poem is ever more than 51 syllables long.

Not haiku or senryu but employing a similar economy, many but not all include one or more *kigo* (season words) to reflect the month of their composition. The first is set in January, the second February, and so on through the years.

TABLE OF CONTENTS

Book I: Stick by stick / 3

Book II: The future tense of warbler was / 41

Book III: A house named Alice / 79

Book IV: Frog asleep / 117

Book V: Should this Stoic chase his hat / 155

Book VI: Like the sun the wind / 193

Book VII: On Watch Hill / 231

Book VIII: Archaeologist of regret / 269

Book IX: Venezuela / 307

36 Views of Fuji

Stick
by
stick

Even savage animals
know better
snarled in their lairs together

we race out into the storm
disentangled from
each other

you go   I come
running after
my words   my white breath

Old groundhog
prognosticator
you never   deliver   spring

from your root-roofed burrow bring
nothing
but shadows

I ask you when will she come again
you answer not
for six more weeks

I cast this line
into the twittering haze

morning sings
before the sun
I left our restless bed

no fish
but longing
bends you

kerplunk

Even more than bird worm
cat bird dog cat
flea the country of dog

I want you conquered
by want I want
you you said

is it two hundred dog years since
your breath yet
a flea in my ear

Stick by stick
the house sparrows knit
the minutes of the long day

this fine rain in
no hurry
to fill the galvanized pail

would that I
could wait for you
so patiently

Lightning bug
the child will clutch
you from the murmuring night

to dissect your
heatless flame
crush you into crumbs of light

Love
let us not waste
rhyme

My dog hikes his leg to sign his name
your husband hoses down
his lawn

your husband sings
the song of the husband this
is mine is mine is mine

I kiss you behind his back
this   the catbird's shadow sings
is mine

Are you of two minds two-flowered
cynthia or do
you   mimic   you

duplicitous   to rule two lovers
to both
to neither

true false dandelion
to thine twin self
true

How many unrepentant falls
since tooth first broke
the apple's skin

careful Adam
cautioned Eve
or I will date myself again

I would drink ruin from your lips
if I knew now
what I know then

Buried summer's snowy notes
the final cricket
faltering

too small a heat
to warm a ghost
in the scrape of wing on wing

he calls   he calls
no one   no one
answering

X's stitch the forest floor
where naked trees
throw down their ghosts

where I find a driven tire
lost in the rime of stream
& stone

Love
where have I traveled to
fall so far from any road

You burst in proud
of the bargains you've found
at the grocery store

snow
a handful of stars winks out
in the midnight of your hair

& I
seduced by your bustle growl
come here

Resolved to love you less
I swear
I will let go your kisses after

no oak hoarding last year's leaves
I will branch bare
among bare branches

I raise my glass to drink to this
& yours is the year's
first laughter

Gulls have folded themselves up
vanes to point the bearings of
the wind

was it such a day as this
I divined you
winter wren

folded you
into my coat
misread your threatening weather

Tonight the zombie opossum
walks
wakes from his living

death to stalk
the blue ice-calving shadows like
an ox-eyed ax

skulks to scare us stiff mid-kiss
an uninvited nearsighted
witness

Cherry pear apple apricot
blossoms make their
promises

this colt
too old
to understand

seeks a breach
in your orchard fence
he'll jump come summer

No vessels ply
the phantom seas
of your dark eye your mouth your hair

O
woman in the summer moon
but I sail there

aloof
deaf
to any distant thunder

I write thunder thunder
struts
as if conjured by the word

lightning likewise
punches cuts
steeples treetops from the murk

four the letters of the word
I don't have the sense to
come in out of

Mother mosquito
interrupts
just as we're about to

she

plays the E
behind the bridge
feeds her violin our blood

a drop of you   a drop of me
beneath her heart
she marries us

I pluck afterward
petals' yellow meteors
from the furrowed bed

scrub your lips
from the lip of your glass & turn
off Chopin mid-nocturne

still
you write when I send you this verse
my mouth bears the bruise of yours

Purple loosestrife
waylays monarchs
to usurp their memories

stays their wings
on their journey home
& they forget how avidly

they sucked the milk-
weed's leaf for bitter-
sweet poison

Children dress up to bewitch us
when they threaten
trick or treat

but we sport no such disguises
play ourselves
come Halloween

I'll be the poet
you'll be muse
costumed in our homespun skin

Rain too late
to green our winter
throats our leaves of grass

are you a masquerade
of summer
come to succor us

or did you mean
to fall in spring
but wet our roots too soon

Ice blinds
idle water
shrouds in dusk

the lake that once
gazed her silence
into us

one last skein of geese
surrenders
earth to her murders of crows

White
that distant
peak through your window

off-white
this palimpsest
I inscribe with this tableau

white
on the bed's bare linen you
doze an indoor drift of snow

Skunk the first
flower of the spring
blossoms in the middle of the road

black white
he blooms a plainer thing
than the crocus purple underground

but O his scent is thunder
no crocus ever dared
to smell so loud

The wind takes liberties
you deny me
hikes your skirt on city streets

the river ogles you & swells
unbuttoned out
in plain sight

& I am jealous of them both
if I lie
I am no robin's son

Death allows us
no deductions
for the kisses we've forgone

refunds not
one minute squandered
making cash in lieu of love

audits in
a mausoleum
our return

My mockingbird incorporates
its tweedle
into his jive & shuck

"honk honk tweet tweet hello
it's a small world
after all"

children spill into the street
to greet the absent
ice cream truck

It   I'm it
the seeker who
hunts you in your hiding place

a backward shadow in the sun
running barefoot
on the grass

as you hide behind your smile
till I find you   tag
you're it

Doubtless it is you
I follow you
to restless water

a silhouette
in the sunlight you
wade into that blinding mirror

I call out for you to turn
back you turn
a stranger

TOMATOES AHEAD
the roadside sign
red paint sprayed on rude plywood

on my way to our assignation
coins of sunlight
pave the road

how'd they know my destination
that I'm thinking of tomatoes
yours

Sea Dogs   0
Thunder   8
moon a powdered sugar-powdered

fried dough
rising O-
ver home plate

might as well be
fan as bat to
wave to each   vacant seat

A straw martyr
on his cross
I have hung the summer long

responsible
for endless corn
I now guard a stubble field

nothing any
self-respecting
crow would want to steal

If you tread upon my shadow
fly asleep
on the windowsill

the world
a leaden tintype of
the world

ferns of ice
upon the glass
dreams of you will wake me

36 Views of Fuji
of the love I've captured
never

still I see it

hover

mirage at the edge of ever

horizon
snowy mountain no
taller than a mound of sugar

The
future
tense
of
warbler
was

Cherry tree
why do you bloom
within the heart of winter

how can I write haiku
when you
blush against nor'easters

pink that cheek of snow for no
good reason
my *kigo*
out
of
season

Fly on the sill
dead since November
stretches exits via window

even reborn yesterday knows
this life is not a room you fill
but

one
you
quit

Palm trees bow to you
the shortstop
as you in a belly-whopper

dive glom the pop-up
& I rounding third for home stop
short as you zip

up button
up my undoing
hit the remote to mute the booing

You lie in bed & listen to
the idling engine of the rain
run

a red-nailed thumb
across my lips & my lips
purse

kiss

whisper when
will we do this again
you laugh   tomorrow   ask me then

The future tense of warbler was
psst
sh sh sh sh sh

warbler in the present is
please
stay still

lastly her past tense will be
ah hell
what sort of warbler was she

Have I caught you
or you me
your inadvertent prey

brushing as I bear you off
your persistent web across
my face

your dinner takes you
out to dinner
spider I'm too horse a fly

We pardon them because they sin
& trespass in
all innocence

for they like we
step thoughtlessly
on the eggs in the nest at the edge

of the pond
where we run splashing in behind
these black smiling dogs

Two lazy naked swimmers we
drift on our raft

the lake in the rain
a hissing pane of glass

the catbird mews & flutes
from his island brake

overhead two vultures spread
their fingers   skate

figure 8s

Even the bluegills
presume you toothsome
nip

the fingertips
you dip into
their sky

they think I'll be worms
you tell me
grin at their mistake

I slip into the pool of heat
you've left
beneath the covers

like a garter snake soak up
the low sun's meanest
heat left over

this bed the rock
on which my soul
would shed its sock of skin

A band of toughs
these chickadees
ditto those bold titmice

hoods
who titter whistle menace us
as we stumble the stark woods

searching for
a place to hide

"when
you're a Jet
you're a Jet
all the way"

Our witless children fancy love
is done with hunger
at our age

that lust deserts the deserts of
the old to rain
upon the young

                fa
               la la
             la la we
            unwrap us
           underneath
              this
              tree

Unfounded this slandering
rain sows a rumor
of you

insinuates in
its purr your murmur
from a dark forsaken room

liar maker
of blind mirrors
of blind mirrors

As a bear grown lean
in his slumber dreams
of food

so do I starve myself
on the twigs of dreams
of you

a fool
under
a Hunger Moon

The wind itself
blows tropes no poet
but the sophomoric would

dances an obituary
page across this
thaw of fossil mud

plasters to my ankles the
fading newsprint faces of
the dead

What has your beauty ever done
to deserve my love
daffodil

& yet I echo you when you
pronounce the one you love
daffodil

I'll be the puddle hungry to
reflect you
April fool

Regarding this fatal
worm versus robin
tug of   war

I root for the robin
who roots for
a subterranean hope

though I've learned
from the worm
this earthy trope

sometimes you must

                        b
                        e

                        t
                        h
                        e

                        r
                        o
                        p
                        e

Here the shy green river house
where first
you shed your clothes

snowy egret at its doorstep
fishing for the
why I let you

go what poet
would not rhyme that
lone white heron with regret

The men who dot this inlet sky
with yellow kites
do not know love

their hobby the sad pastime of
the strung wish
the chaste meanwhile

they plant their feet on sand fix
their advertisements on the off-
shore wind

Because the mountain
won't I will
move to the mountain

where I & the evening
grosbeak will
gild your blinded windows

monadnock
knock
at your locked back door

I look you up in The Book of Rivers
find you under
Milky Way

note nobody is recovered
who has swum your
fiery waters

this day
the day
that night deposes day

Like the moon
like blue jay's blue
I live on borrowed light

would be
without you
leaden feathers under ashen skies

or but a planet's shadow
occulting stars
transiting the night

A fox among houses
lost in the city
a maze of wire fences

run how did I come to
run how did I come to
run to be here

leash your dog
cup his eyes
until my bewildered heart slips

out of time

Coy at the mirror
you in your bra
wink as I take this picture of

you making eyes at me
        as I catch
you making eyes at me

wink as I take this picture of
you in your bra
Coy at the mirror

I believed that you would be
as constant as
the sun

born the morning of each day
to thaw the icebound earth
again

but now I know that even day
will break
its promises

Now where was I going the
hedge a
calliope

sparrow
sparrow
sparrow you

land beside me on this branch
beneath us
planet

    s
     w
      a
       y

Spring that demonstrative lover
checks in
to the room next door

lugs in her baggage of
squalls & squeaks
of birds of frogs of cats in heat

& we with our TV
on why don't we

SHRIEK

No
I never loved you never
never told you

so
never once did I surrender
never let you

go
never ached to hold you never
played this April Fools' Day joke

Remember me?
the catbird asks
wings on his hips on my doorstep

home to cool New England from
his hot Guatemalan
winter

I'd like a bite
of your white pear
sometime this summer

Already lilies
rouse to lap our
sweat & bow to lick

their pollen stuck
to our bodies
tawdry orange lips

yawn to gargle
any dowsing
insect

In this blue dream
we are discovered
in flagrante delicto

two seen sawing
summer's burning
grass as grass-

hoppers saw their
two- no triple-time
anti-ant fandangos

One too precocious tree
I
glow against the green

blushing
like a McIntosh
in the Dog Star's dawn

but then I'm always
when it comes to
love the first to fall

Dusk a black & agile moon
rose on the rust
of starlings' wings

which whistling laid
its darkness down
upon the shoulders of this world

no I needed no new moon
to tell me love's
the end of all

Summers we make fast
our hammock
from the willow to the ash

it is the riddled boat we promise
we will pilot
but we lie

let it drift a derelict
until at last it swamps with yellow
leaves

This white gate in
this bare wood closed
letting no one into nowhere

who does it stop you ask
this gate alone
with no fence to interfere
with our trespass here

now I push you hip to latch
answer   let me in

Not that bourbon ever wrote
one thing
worth a damn

but on this the longest night
as water thins its burning in
my glass

it writes "she loves you not"
it writes *"in vino veritas"*
it writes this

A house named Alice

To hear your heart
its liquid tick
I press my ear against your breast

klepsydra
thief of water
prisoned in the cage of your chest

minutes flow
below the ice
one kiss makes your clock run fast

Lusting for a living leaf
I hang around
each nursery

hothouse cold frame
greenhouse to
eyeball winter's refugees

I thumb Burpee's catalogs
for porn
of the garden variety

You ask me if my eyes are not
stuck
upon your tattered photograph

blind to any
but the pose you struck
some twenty-seven Marches back

but no

you dazzle my eyes still
still the reckless
beauty of your past

My sixty-fourth spring
& I still can't figure
out how she pulls that

mourning dove out of
an unin-
habited hat

to sough
wu
on the green ash branch

Crossing the road
to help her cross
I turn into the turtle

cars blur   I pull
my suddenly retractable
head in

to breathe within
the painted stone
holding her breath in my hands

Today I shall think
of the small
of your back

as you lie
on white sand
your dark eyes shut fast

& too the small tears
of sweat
pooling there

A house named Alice
FOR SALE
here beside a jealous sea

ah Love she could be
our cedar-shingled summer palace
I tease

but you say no
you know we'd never
rest in her embrace

You are countless miles away
but I can sense you
sailing off this coast

half expect you
to be borne on a beryl wave
Venus of the Boats

but these low breakers only bring
spent sand dollars
bottles wanting notes

At my at-bat
you warmed up your arm to strike me
OUT

you flung I swung &
summer's end
sent a startled harbinger

lost in the lights a great horned owl
swept through the outfield
blind as a ball

Yesses never
quick
as noes

each day you do not
answer
heartens me

I wait
zealously
Linus hunkered among his pumpkins

Like me the great
black-backed gull
is shackled to desire

his find a fat
blue mackerel
too ample to devour

he would take flight
but lack will pull
him downward to despair

When sparrows land
their shadows fly
to meet them

I am a skiff
you are the wind
I run before

who was the wit
who wrote this shit
in my padlocked diary

The memories no longer
come to my summons
but of their own will

recall themselves
awakened by
some   other   one

a jay will loose
that snow-bowed bough
scolding

someone for something

Woodpecker circles
woodpecker
circles woodpecker

a beaks-up downy
do-si-do
around a hollow trunk

from this I draw
no conclusions
whatsoever about us

Instinct is
the name we give
the thing we can't explain

two ducks we've christened
John & Mary
rendezvous in our yard each spring

instinct we explain
which like the name of love does not
explain a thing

This day we must surrender
love
& then what have we left

the wrens'
at our shuttered windows
peekaboo
peekaboo
peekaboo

we should have been preparing for
we were not prepared for
this

Nobody speaks
of moth does not
also speak of flame

& yet he must
before he burns
burn to mix his ash with hers

else we wingless
ones would find us
minus one cliché

Big as she
the robin bugs
his mother till she stuffs

down his pinching
throat a spray of
gold legs scissoring

so does another
grasshopper
enter heaven's kingdom

& what had love
what had our lust
to do with honesty

fireworks blind the stars' dim eyes
it is the light you
it is the dark I

see

I stole this trope from another
honestly

Skip   ping
that   flat
rock

a
cross the river's twitchy back
you told me no we can't

stop
we stop we
drown

Nine minutes
of your sighs are still
inside my pocket-sized recorder

your slow speeding up of breath until
you laugh & cry out
all at once

one word
"stop"
tucked in my pocket

From the stars
to flesh our dreams
we manufacture skeletons

constellations
asterisms
the great bear's tail & hip

these signs exist
do not exist
to help us lose our way

Nothing lasts forever nothing
silences
me

in May I write November
why must I write November
in May

birds don't
keep speaking after
birds have nothing left to say

As if this night
the north wind cricks
its phantom limbs

the scarred oak in
my chest of drawers
groans

to share my careful
sleep my bones
knotted in these tangled clothes

Walking backward
in my tracks
that I might end in trackless snow

or that whoever
follows me
might think so

I cross the dark-eyed junco's path
& where she stops
find me   lost

Twice shy burned once
not I the slow learner who
can't not touch a hot stove

ever sure to be love's dunce
last kid in class
to get the lesson of

      A your glance
    + B your pout
    = C you later

Big Boy

Bleeding heart
jets
you

overnight
express
to

spring
one blossom
long

Accidental
my glance
catching on this vivid splinter

winter's blue hills
smile pink
through the trees

looking out
my bedroom window
I must remember to forget you

Paws tucked under
himself the cat
will not even blink

as we as hungry as
two claws
unsheathe each other

don't worry he
can't tell on us

cat's got his tongue

Touch-me-not
you are no more
yellow for my saying so

beauty being
beauty you
do not need my songs

& yet my touch
on your shy petals
spurs such blue ejaculations

Half moon you are
one half of me
pale traveler beside me

& yet
our life together is
but two lives apart

& yet
you always follow as
I welcome grass for pillow

Time casts no shadow
to tell this
straitened hour

sundial
blinded
by a fold of morning fog

like a blade this gnomon would
bared to clean sun
sunder us

From here the mountain
is so far
you can eclipse it with your thumb

& you who always loved me less
with one fillip
could make it tumble

from here it is   but a solitary bluff
our lives
escape us

Before I became this poem
I was the woebegone
poet's lunch

am
the transubstantiation of
wine & cheese & ham

& these
seventeen syllables seventeen delectable
sour grapes

I'd like to thank
the language
especially the words who

helped me chip
this flint into
a leaf to tip my spear

that I might deliver
the happy beast to cheer you
some glum time

So at last we come to this
the long lost Odysseus
home

no I am no hero am
the washed-up castaway
who apes him

& this the bed
that I have made
of love's stuttering progress

Frog
asleep

Juncos return
my heart
kicks up thistle

seeds from the snow
quick backward
jumps to

the vernal pool of you
iced in
in this
our false spring's overthrow

Frog asleep
beneath
the pond

the sound

of snow

    f
    a

    i
    n
    g

on snow

What was it brought them here today
these pint-sized duck impersonators

this raft of stubby scuffed black shoes
that bobs this brackish stretch of river

coots
coots
coots
coots
like them we build our house on water

Spring cleaning I find
the barrette I once found
in my disheveled bed

unfasten the clasp
your untarnished brass
fasten it on empty air

O how have you gone
with your wild hair undone
even these forty years

A ghost of your kiss visits my lips
wings of a moth
beating my mouth

& this is how I woke in your arms
in the tousled bed
of our youth

& this is how I wake from a dream
old & alone
with that truth

As one blind I trace

the deep defile
the gentle vale
the white-sand abandoned isle

of your breasts
your spine
your hip

as one blind   as your voice
on the telephone
assumes your shape

The surgeons split me like a fish
to reconstruct
my failing heart

now   stumbling   scarred
so soon fulfilled
I can tell   for all their practiced art

upon these plumbed & buttressed pipes
they failed to fix
the br ken part

Meteors fell
a rain of light
on the night that I was born

a fallen
Perseid
grandson of a quondam god

Earth's late visitor
buckled into this carcass for
the long ride home

As I would rid me of my sins
I cast this bread
upon the waters

to feed the fish my sinfulness
one bite-sized bit
for each blue kiss

fishes should redeem my fate
expunge each kiss
each bite they ate

At the window you say
look
come come look at the moon

but I am writing this book
I'm writing I murmur
soon

what is the moon to my book

& you
what is your book to the moon

The spirits rocking
in the rocking
chairs on our chill porch

are but the wind
you say as we
divide our heat indoors

O no I say
my Love do not
presume to blame the wind

Falling down this mountain
on two wheels we
skirt the lip of the abyss

on every hairpin turn we make
but pull no brakes as we
fall

ten thousand feet to ground
& the wish that we
could fall

forever

down

I remind you of your vow to burn
unread
my ragged diaries

those boxes upon boxes of
journals kept
since I turned thirteen

not to save my memories
but to save your memory
of me

If I dared to orchestrate
my songs
no practiced band would dare to play

but the black-eyed susans slumbering
beneath this snow'd be
wrenched awake

by tyros tuning   toy instruments
that never shared the selfsame
A

Stranger   friend   lover
it is the other makes us one

I fall awake
shapeless under

this daydreaming Worm Moon
but even her blind gaze will do

you are my help
I'll be your help

we force each other   into form

Always I pulled dandelions
always
they grew back

my mother
who commanded this
said I must pull up the roots

but how could a child
reach them when
they stretched all the way to

China

Even the beetle
going about his business
you make your toy

put down your hand
lift him from the walk
let him trickle across your palm

but when he gains the edge you
twist your wrist
allow no arrival

There was a time
the stars would come
down from their homes in summer

to telegraph their dreams in Morse
from cold green lanterns
in the grass

but those were the nights
I was a child
before our lamps erased their eyes

Remember when we stripped to swim
in the dry creek bed
& then

scrambled headlong
up its banks
clutching clothing to our breasts when

in two straight lines
around the bend
marched a wide-eyed Cub Scout troop

Bees won't
I have been told
sting if you stay

still as a rose
& so I freeze
as your fingers stroll

the prickly stem of my blooming throat
& hope I will
& hope you won't

We almost miss these visitors
their color the color
of the sand

the yellowlegs   the plovers
who fly from us
across blue waters

of our home Narragansett Bay
where we too
are just passing through

Ancient black piano
at the picture window

you in your sheer red
shift ply the yellowed

keys till they
glow   white   hot

your naked silhouette
in the window's light

plays blues to make a
black piano blush

Gods Absent Month
the cold earth's cup
pours out its abundance of birds

even the piebald trees
have shed
their gaudy fluttering tongues

& I

       am   the
      last   goose
        in   line
           on   the
             starboard   wing
                    of   the
                      V

7:30 thirty-six
hours away from you

I live in dreams
this deathless night
of our fated rendezvous

we've waited twenty years
you say
what's another hour

another hour's another
twenty years

雀
suzume inscribed in me
this kanji names my muse

this electric needle
sews
its black track into

my arm that I may wear unto
my death your heart
upon my sleeve

The girl in the photograph
my unsmiling mother
clutches a ball

her dark eyes measure
the distance to
the photographer

sleep   dear ashes   sleep
once you were unleashed
you could never be recalled

Asking the stone angel
to tell me
how to leave her

each night I paced
among
the flickering graves

until the night the angel
stepped down
from his pedestal

When starling fell
down the flue
into my famished hearth

that unwitting prisoner
fled my hand
bared to free her

how is it you
preferred your cell
to your would-be rescuer

What makes you think
the gods are out
to do us any favors

there's many a god
who would as soon
slit your throat as look at you

our lives   their TV
our loves   their novels
our wars   their sport

War is won
says Master Sun
by leading the foe astray

near you must seem far
far	near
able	helpless
ready	unprepared

to take the eager enemy
we engage unclad

A soldier in the sort of war
that ends
in mutual surrender

Ovid banished to the shore
of the Black Sea
writes

"here to spin love poems is
to sing to the deaf
to sign to the blind

Here at the HOME
of the
WORLD FAMOUS
HOT WIENER OMELET

I am the same
world famous poet
breaks his fast on anything but

even the moon
knows better
than to stay up all night

I always end up
on the hard bench
outside the principal's office

how can I help it when
I goggle watching you
sharpen your pencil

swoon in the wake of your
scent swirling after you
sway past my desk

The bay asleep
that slate afternoon

as gulls napped on their shadows &
geese snoozed on placid glass

your big red ship came
churning from the city
rumbling into voyage

your big blue wake woke
every   body   up

I am the accidental
bird blown off course

the cuckoo
in Rhode Island who

lost his way

cuckoo who
smacks into
your bedroom window

stunned by that suddenly

solid air

Someone's tied a scarf upon
the nude statue
in the storm

she's still in her birthday suit
but at least her neck
is warm

when you left you left behind

your scent

your promise

winter

Should
this
Stoic
chase
his
hat

We call our nuthatch Mr.
as if he were
an honored guest

whose yank-yank proclamations we
accord our highest regard

for upside down & bare he braves
to the bitter
end this endless winter

Should this Stoic chase his hat
or calmly watch
wind win it

swathe himself against the gale
or stroll naked
in it

take no drink of your hard love
or fall down drunk
this minute

March comes in like a
something
you say

& goes out like a
something else
I reply

some birds walk
some birds hop
it makes no nevermind to the worm

One year quits us in one day

we wake to spring's shy sun
the morning lake

swim a summer thunderstorm
in the river noon

drink on the ocean
fall's keen bite at dusk

one year one day
our winter   just ahead of us

Birds sleep with open eyes to see
that stars don't stray
from their constant paths

long white lines of light
their dreams
circumscribed upon the black

but our eyes fold into themselves
as poppies do
late afternoon

My first bride tripped
on the hem of her dress
ripped it down   popped out her breasts

nose-dove   planted   her face in the cake
the knife in her hand
de trop

the perfect wedding memory
that perfectly wed catastrophe

You are off to visit
your beloved sister

call the dancing girls
I tell the cat
hooray it's party time

then we

loaf   on the sofa
chew   lukewarm pizza
& ogle

HGTV's
new
Dream Home Design

Father & mother of waves
we fear
they will break

like green Depression glass

they are after all all motion
breath moving through them
they themselves

still

we deliver them to the sea

return to us
& pray they will

A difference engine
the grasshopper calculates

the angle to

leap
to escape my narrow step

"all the while sleep
shares our lives with us"

pace Seneca

my window proves nothing but
blue mackerel sky

Old dog
you will become
that bush you used to piss upon

this fur this bark this tail
I tell
is you   wearing   you

but when I point this out to you
you point to
the looking glass

We know a kind of pale distress
in this
our chronic parting

although we undertake to do
our best
to mask it   fecklessly

you make a face
I make a joke
       "Drive wrecklessly"

Waving my wings
like an unfledged bird
I dive beak-first

into the ice

this my last & first
try skating
kids dancing camels

around me

I strapped these blades
to these splayed feet
to chase you across this pond

How come when
Dr. Zhivago lifts a pen
balalaikas play

whereas when
I wield *my* pen
like a conductor's baton all day

crickets

She disappears   into herself
folds inward
with her folding bones

pleats the plane to seal herself
in squash blossom   rue petal
rabbit's ear

I wish wishes could unfold her
my origami
paper daughter

Sun's up   drunk red
dawn on River Road
damn him   damn his eyes

birds chirp singsong
songs eternal sung
damn them damn their eyes

spring's sprung   this young
nincompoop in love
damn me   damn my eyes

[sic]

The day before yesterday
you asked me
did you fill the beedfirder

yesterday you said
about the cat
sometimes he's an askhole

that bird book says that bird's got
pale underpants
you inform me today

Could we have thought
we would not be changed
utterly by love

bobolinks banjo
above the budding fields
can't stop slopping

the tongue-tied skies
with lovesick musick
O could we

A lonely sparrow follows you
as you in your garden
dig up grubs

face dirt-blurred
you serve his supper on
the board of our winding walk

where he hops
& watches & hopes
for a dollop of succulent grub

Clams on the strand
on this blue day

we walk through them in tandem

some we save
throw back
to the waves

some we leave
for the gulls
to crack

we laugh to think our fate will be
as random

The moonflower is our instructor
who teaches the art of delay

who waits to the wane of summer
who waits to the ebb of the day

for the sun to succumb to shadow
for the hummingbird moth to stray

To the birds
you raised your glass & winked
to the birds I concurred & drank

as we had made
of them our code
for private thoughts in a public place

those two blue herons we gave flight
were they two
or the same one twice

The mower edged the flowerbed
his purpled scythe
a shear dis-

aster

in his distraction beheaded them
& marvelled at
now   aimless   bees

so do I grieve
as he to grass
so do you   to me

A young man mad
about art

dipped a chicken's
feet in red paint

chased it
across a blue arc
brushed on paper

named his painting

*Red Maple Leaves
on the Tatsuta River*

& so would I swim
in this floating world

After you had set me free
you told me to read
your page one story

about a captured
crow named Charlie
set free in the naked wood

your last line

   "You never know when
     a fair wind
   might bring him back"

Who cares the dead
may sing my praises
& their fine dust honor mine

will my bones then bow
& blush & flushed with fame
sign my autograph

or perhaps the birds grown fat
on worms grown fat on me
will tweet my name

Prostate biopsy
as the doctor shoots
needles up my asshole

Frank Sinatra croons
Fly Me to the Moon
on the radio

God-in-Heaven's got one hell
of a cackling sense of
humor

The first day of spring delivers
winter's
heating bill

the ice cream parlor opens
its dreaming doors
to snow

& the bare trees blush
like flirting girls
in Hopeville

I learned too late
he died too soon

his staunch heart
surrendering

for forty years
my friend who spoke

of nothing but love
that mattered

at our last date
at the Indian lunch buffet

for Patrick William Murphy

This spiderless web
next to the birdhouse
sign of a bad decision

I spent twenty bucks
on Carl Sandburg's book
my what a bad decision

hunger builds webs
plucks them clean

I was caught starving
for something to read

It's said trees remember
& speak to each other
of all that passes

beneath

does that tree on campus
gossip still
of the night you   siren

told me to lean
against its skin
& you knelt on the earth before me

I'll wear my cats-launching-rockets
Hawaiian shirt
this 4th of July

if I want to
goddamnit
because *I'm* an American & *proud*

of that accident
don't need your OK to make
an ass   of myself

Certainly we cannot know
the thing-in-itself
but why

should we care
aboard this foundering scow
among *les fous de Bassan*

where the dirty sea captain
nuzzling the French girl's
nape is just that

I follow your bottom
up the stairs
a perk I say of courtesy

perhaps you say
but the honest reason
men invented chivalry

I open my door
let you in
give thanks for
the artfulness of men

Your face its delicate machinery
its seven valves
open

membranes lenses musculature
tuned to the movements
of other souls

usefully employed
in the manufacture
of masks

So that our lust might last forever
we pledge we'll always
live apart

our eyes won't weary
of each other
the mundane creatures that we are

but safe to share this
Mourning Moon
for we'll be thirty   earths apart

G-A-G-E-C-A-G
a cat's-paw plucked
on our wind chimes clear

did you see
you asked
did you hear
we might wait ten thousand years

for a random breeze to play again
Ru-dolph-the-red-nosed-rein-deer

Like
the
sun
the
wind

These dismal afternoons I spend
alone
alone go to my bed

wake to find you dreaming there
but I must go & dare not
wake you

two strangers who were lovers
once
we spend our nights alone together

You kiss the livid cicatrix
the sutured fissure
to my heart

the pale shades of staples run
down its dis-
jointed spine
like jointed
legs

but I am ice
& I know that ice
by sun & moon will heal itself

But I would not relinquish you
even when
you would go dark

now each new day
holds minutes more
daylight than the day before

when you halve
a centipede
its several severed legs keep r u n n i n g

Ponytail swinging
the jogger accosts me

tells me to call upon
Jesus I say right you betcha

good she says & beams
deaf to scorn

turns
jogs off

her name in green emblazoned on
her black spandexed back:

GOD

Wooden box propped
on the stick

attached to the string
attached to the carrot

never caught a rabbit

no matter
how often I set it

the only thing trapped
was the rabbit's laugh

Like the sun the wind
casts shadows

betrayed by its fingers in the sand
after beachgrass

the leaves that huddle to heap themselves
east of your house

face the wind

feel its shadow at your back
close   as your lover's absence

Every road is a cul-de-sac
that takes me
to the sea

& I who should know better drive
again   again
to each dead end

here

on your island

on which I cannot live
& which I cannot leave

I look into your face your eyes
white as the gull
blue as the wave

the hand of the wind lifts your hair
& I taste the salt spray on your lips

high on the hill the windows watch
they witness us
the houses

Cape Ann

How many grow wheat
to feed hungry mouths

how many translate
their earth to coin & paper

as for me   my crop is sparrows
their beaks chanting plainsong

my harvest hollows in the dirt
their deserted dusty baths

Carving the pumpkin
I joked of how I
would plagiarize your eyes

           jack
            o'
          lantern

I should have known better
than to try
to catch you   falling knife

Earthworms as fat as mice
turned up under
the leaves I raked

squirmed alarmed
till I freed them to
sew themselves into the earth

just as I will the happy lies
I've told myself
in my diaries

Saw in hand in freezing rain
I searched
to find the one

the chosen found
I knelt down
on my knees in the mud

hands thick with sap
face a numbed mask
saw   binding in the wood

Old house you say
as if that were an answer

the soft coat made
of our shed skins

our dust furs surfaces
to turn furniture feral

my hand a rag
to strip its sift

your hide to ford
our deepening winter

Don Quixote a cello
stumbling

Sancho Panza a viola
bumbling after

asking
will we remember

when the voices of birds
were a plucking of strings

river a bow
seesawing above

a bridge

Is that you junco
still kicking the yellow
grass on the roof of hell

soon the Sugar Moon
will deliver her shadow
a round cloud of birds

my fingers   will feather
bones   will hollow
face   taper   to a thorn

Lousy with robins
spring muscles on
singing such slovenly lovesongs

red-wing's bubble
flicker's drum
finch's cavil
catbird's cat's meow

the wood wood wood thrush his
Paleozoic fugitive jazz

Trafficking in the masks of birds
second person
even third

I steal their voices
to speak through
the safe remove of "he" & "you"

I need long water
to take off
which makes me a common loon

Across the street
from my blue house
a yellow backhoe bites the earth

the air today
is amniotic
a gravid sky gives summer birth

a blue tent   yellow lilies
a last home
for my new neighbor

Beaks bleeding ketchup
the panhandling gulls
mocked Hitchcock extras

as the

sun fried the French girl
ketchup red she drowned her
French fries in ketchup fed

the gulls

as her red bikini deliquesced
into her ketchup knolls

You sit up in the treetop cat
for the hook & ladder

thrilled by your
speed up the blur of leaves

& shriek of blue jay's dive
into

the sky's blue water never
thought how you would ever

get down

Convinced my sinister
hand would betray me
my grandmother

who raised me
broke me of its use
& taught my right to write true verse

Grandma if you only knew
the dextrous wrong
that right can do

Dog in a boneyard
I glide a smiling
ghost among the stones

lost in a net of scents
thrown across the grass
I dig for my bones

know my soul will never be
as good & plain & naked as
your own

Like a biplane badgering
King Kong
one skinny fly buzzes me

a summer leftover
in chill November
he circles sluggishly

but I stay my swatter
I need a friend to
spend the winter with me

The paint-by-numbers sky today
is 2
the clouds are 3

your eyes your hair
are 9 beneath
the number 13 trees

71
must be a typo
your heart forever 17

With a flick of your wrist
you can make the cat dance
stripped to his stripes

in his cat underpants
up on his hind legs
he bats at the wire

all we can say
for that thing called desire
aka   this fine romance

I sneeze in my room

& my ukuleles thrum

hung on these walls

they breathe with me

such sympathetic wood

    to my

lungs & bones & blood

they   play   me

Stopping off for fast food
on their long drive home
submarine mergansers

punk mohawks flattened
shoot the yellow shallows
like long-necked torpedoes

a thousand frogs jump out
  the pond

     the sound

          of scram

You chew out your daffodils
for dallying
while others' bloom

pep talk peonies
discipline Scotch broom
coax the roses from their canes

pronounce the dandelions' doom
my mud-smudged lover
my without whom

Ever since that pretty girl
in seventh grade
borrowed my eraser

I've erased my life to love
the much mistaken girls
who move

to the desk
beside my desk & will ask
to borrow my eraser

Curled inside
each egg-shaped stone

a bird

sun snug
here on the lip of the sea

hold it to your ear
& you will hear it

sing you said
when you were thirteen

Guests can enjoy
the motel's basketball hoop"
said the Stardust on its

website
site of our last rendezvous
where I unwitting as a joke

gave you a basketball
spanking-new
a gift   to the end of us

I am but an amateur
practitioner of grief
one untrained

in the tools of the trade
what good are tears
if they cannot bring relief

what use this heart
a thing so poorly made
that one goodbye could

As you described your epiphany
the great blue heron
on the dock

how he strode to the end on chopstick legs
looked down the lake
scissored back

pivoted
stalked out again
I saw myself the idle ghost of him

My fair-haired son at three
remembers
the night he died

with Zack & Zakie
his twin siblings
& their father their

blue van rolled

over where

on a map of LA county
he points to the spot & tells me
"There"

Of wine it's said Li Po could get
one hundred lines
per bottle

a poem
at the bottom
every cup

drove drunk

our fierce embraces
cloud the windows
I drive blind   inside your breath

I promise you I will return
but I can not
restore

for I am banished from myself
even as I close
this door

as I the river   step into
the one I was I am
no more

On Watch Hill

First memory
four sparrows
    crying in the snow

mother's shadow holds me
from the doorway throws
    out a slice of toast

four sparrows at four corners
lift it   off it goes
hopping
    down
        the
road

As one put drunk into the Packet-boat
I am translated to

this
nether shore

like Tom May wake to wonder how
my lost name will find me

if eyes could see through this blear air
I would indite no

broken poems

Today I am a loose flock
of souls
a slack confederation of

my countless thousands
of remembered &
forgotten lives

odd thoughts
of my iterations
as I walk into my evening

Our wakes on the lake
the same V shape

our reflections take
in flight

always a lone sentinel
to mind us

        & when
at rush hour

we single-file cross
traffic stops

& nobody not a goose
                honks

Over the pale hills
under a wool sky
you were the rain on my tongue

rain
as sharp as the peach's pit
as fecund as estuary mud

rain to run
down the holes in my roof
even the new moon can't plumb

Wallace Stevens bought next door
a house in Hartford
near the park

someone should have warned
his neighbors
we poets never mow our yards

now his neighbors
curse his grass
as Wallace turns into a blackbird

A child I caught them in a jar
fireflies' ascent

now sit up in bed to catch
fireflies only dreamt

woke to
wake to

insects dead in a jelly jar
lyrics dead in a book unkempt

You send me Benny Goodman
I quick slip off
the cardboard cover

forever hoping for an answer
but I hear only
that ghostly

thinking reed's
cool tootle
on a hot dead night in Carnegie Hall

A tree on fire undresses
sheds its burning leaves
at the Valvoline

a fat man waddles out
to blow out the leaves
at the Valvoline

when all the trees go naked
your hair smells like leaves
at the Valvoline

Lord Bow-Wow & Lady Meow
Santoka wrote
had come from nowhere

the white dog who gave him
the black rice cake
the cat he gifted after

messengers to his One-Grass Hut
that fall he fell
           dragonfly drunk

No killdeer I
would break my wing
when I could feign it broken

I swept us clean as this spit of land
dune grass where our house
used to stand

the only sign we ever were
red bricks waveworn
in the sand

Pantless Santa living free
or dying in New Hamster

burly cops hurled candy he
paraded through New London

who the hell
are you

you asked the acned Santa who
brought your new two-wheeler

Still
this
third-floor walk-up

still
Bank Street
at dawn

till
the razor you
rocked in its cradle

fell
long after
you'd gone

The weather soothsayer
augurs oobleck

the frowning announcer
smiles as the news

segues from
massacres to laxatives

for each fresh kill
there's a feel-good story

thank Zeus

Worse than the spider
on the ceiling the spider
magically gone

where is she where is she
takin' a bath don't wanna

be

pounced

on

>   (I spurn spiders
>   you snub snakes
>   any with too many
>   or too few legs)

Thirteen when I snuck aboard
a boxcar bound for
Colorado

rode beside the Pink Moon till
she hid behind blue mountains

where I bathed in snowmelt streams
quaked
with the aspen

I don't know this didn't happen

The petals pressed into my journals
yellow shadows
on the page

where I   to record our rendezvous
wrote but the numbers
of our rooms

that tell all
in telling nothing
we hid our trysts behind close walls

Our room so dark
our skin
our eyes

what do we know
of the world
beyond us

blind as we are
as tactile as
mussels in a tidal pool

Our children go feral
summer vacations
animals barely clothed

yell "car!" as they play
in the heart of the street
walk an invisible

dog down the beach
quick   catch them quick
as they caw caw like crows

Fifty years I saw not one
then in one day I see fifty

bluebirds

perhaps what I never saw
was there to witness

all along

who has ever even seen
one-fiftieth

of the world before him

Paula Red Northern Spy
not a middle reader but
two pomes we seek

to relive our primal sin
on this
our fallen orchard walk

ah   a blushing Fuji
I stretch   wish me brave enough
tiptoe   to   pluck

Blue rivers in my father's hands
beneath skin's mottled parchment
swell

the unrelenting rain of days
will wash away
his earth   his fall

bare his roots
bare his bones
the buried child   beneath the sill

As trees shed their clothes
we disappear
into hats & coats & gloves

& yet your lips
thaw to my kiss

& I think to drink my
tropes from your mouth
map from your breath

the Way

After the sun
the pine trees cast

pine-shaped
shadows of snow

white arrow heads
shades on the grass

point north

to our sly afternoon's
swiftly gathering past

Preachers said I had to choose
whiskey or
my soul's salvation

water to wine
I chose the divine
faith you buy in a bottle

if you have ever walked this world
you know God didn't
build it sober

Drunk on endorphins
I love the talk
of men in the locker room

naked hairy bears at ease
to confess
their embarrassments

Mike where've you been
I put on weight
I was ashamed
ah   Mike   that's OK

On Watch Hill
Halley's Comet
flowers far above the rain

we've come miles to miss
this apparition
we won't live to see again

what else should these blind bones do
but run blind drunk
into the waves

That apple tree I planted
last fall
laughs

tall & thin
a teenager
taller than
his gray stepfather

his white laughter augurs
perhaps apples
perhaps pomes

penyeach

Lyin' in bed
all knuckles & knees

hear the birds talkin'
in the coconut trees

don't wanna listen to
that kinda talk

bones in my body gotta
get up & walk

got the 4-in-the-mornin'
birds-up blues

Like children playing Statues
spun & flung apart
we freeze where we fall

called upon to name ourselves
what are you   & what am I
after all

beyond the end of this brief affair
no key to these
dark offices

Every lost place I go
your shadow
runs beside me on my path

a small winged thing
dark at my feet
oaring over this black earth

I stop
& lift my eyes to heaven
& hold my hopeless breath

Leaves in your panties
leaves in your hair
on this forest floor

as I take you here
your mouth my mouth
to use as I please

but what will you tell
your jealous husband
when you like an oak shed

leaves

Kingfisher teach me
to live without her

as I would teach you
to fly without wings

all that I have
is nothing to give

to your rattling laugh
in the arms of the trees

no door but the one
you open to me

Wang Wei taught this
song of longing
you lost to me for so many years

warrior of the heart
gone to fight
so far away in so many wars

I should have told you
as he would
to send a sign with each wild goose

Me lacking sea legs
I stumble to stand
on this wildly tilting floor

this no ship & on no water
but there you stand
still ravishing as

you were twenty years
before I can speak you
throw my heart overboard

*As well fall in love with a sparrow
that flies past
& is gone from sight*

love not the frail things of this world
Marcus warns
        but then what shall we love

ask I the half-assed Stoic
who gives to a sparrow
                his sparrow heart

Archaeologist of regret

The rope
when he found the photograph
he asked only about the rope

not your knowing *post hoc* smile
nor the blush on your bare breast
but the rope

perhaps it was he'd never hoped
to find his love bound
by another

Of course we always thought
we would come back to this

to the true trade winds
gusting with the waves' white

roar through our cabin

to the brown pelicans
headlong crashing in the bay

of course we always
thought we could come back

South Water Caye
Belize

Wrong longitude
your dead reckoning
runs me aground in open seas

no help from
the moons of Jupiter
who do not have the time for me

you've left my riven hull a phantom
on land where no land
should be

The year's first heron lifts
his gray sails to steer his ship
low over me

the deep keel
of his streaked breast bone
his black feet
the tiller after

I ache to follow
leave this earth to go
wherever he is going

In no way will I think that
we
are the betters of the birds

in fact I think the opposite
for
they boast the better words

than we the leaden statues
who
can't understand each other

On their hands & knees they walk
whine   dine   9 o'clock

in Dogtown you said

moonbathe   && howl the sun
sniff each others' butts when done

you wound your arm around your head
& this is how they scratch their ears

in Dogtown you said

for J

Snapshot 1935
George Oppen aboard
the Galley Bird

casts his grin upon
the summer Sound
as he reefs sail

off New London

fixed in our arrogant present
we too dream of
no moment after

Lost!
forgotten with your blindfold
in the dresser drawer

of a hotel room
on the coast of Maine
for housekeeping staff to find

no doubt to be but
one more rope to
bind their boundless collection

& so you have come back to me
your old teacher
school begun

is there even one instruction
I have to save you
even one

step outside
be the wind
name a bird   get to know him

I take you out   buy you a pair
of fuck-me pumps
   fire-red 5-inch
            he
            el
             s

then
we hit the raw bar
drink oysters   eat our
iced martinis dry

precarious-
ly tall now
the first time
you can   look me in the
eye

Humerus
not humorous
my pratfall in the park

watching the geese
instead of my feet
lands me a broken arm

now how can you laugh at that
I'm all fall
& no prat

Bill Shakespeare's mistress never dug
his sonnets a quid
I'll wager

understanding
better than he
how poems are but a vanity

O hell Bill
you're scribbling still
it's Christmas bring your bloody bones to bed

Friends go on vanishing
steadily stepping off
the edge of the earth

& as they wait for us
the crows
breathe   snow   smoke

planet's end
just a step away
in any direction you look

Three crows eat
someone for breakfast
exit 1   I-395

day 1		flesh
day 2		bones
day 3		rain
day 4

big snapping turtle
leaves his house of water
slogs the road's cold shoulder

When you go out
you lock me in
so I'll be safe at my desk upstairs

or is it just
so I won't escape
your key to keep me writing here

that grackle walks
you say
he walks   like a bowlegged cowboy

With their furniture of grass & twigs
my new tenants
are moving in

to the room I've framed for them
on the post beside
my side porch step

should I the brand-new landlord fret
I've yet to get
        their first month's rent

Not another word
swear to God I'll kiss your mouth
shut

swore the minute that you walked
through that door
I'd take you

first
    (no time for second thoughts)
let's pull up that skirt

Catbird in the birdbath bathes
hikes her grave
chemise

shimmies   shakes
sluices   waves
slate fallen feather navies

drinks to quench her thirst
your thirst my thirst our quenchless
thirst

Chirring heart buried
in burrs of the thicket

chirks like the cynic hinge
of a dry & gutless bucket

sprawls on the swells
of the summer air

yellow-breasted chat perhaps
or just another fool making racket

Archaeologist of regret
I prized you from
your maker's grip

where ten thousand years you'd slept
in that slim basket of bones
his fist

sought to tame you tameless yet
my graven sparrow
gravely missed

Of our stolen hours you ask
which instant does
my heart love best

before   I say   we dare to kiss
but our tongues
all words arrest

for then we breathe each other's breath
& all our doubts
are dispossessed

You haunt a host of houses
the nosy ghost the owners
never see

your virtual visitations to
their bedrooms baths
& water views

do come home I say as you
barnstorm their gardens
like a bumble bee

When I die
do not confess
the things that we have done

our love should end
as cleanly as
we end when I am gone

our wishes lies & secrets are
to tell
the dead alone

Winter I save seven
seeds
within my paper skin

the seven words
you wrote to me
impatient to be sown

"I want to
kiss you
in summertime"

Watch yourself as if you were
one who waits in ambush to
take your life

Epictetus tells us
& indeed I know
no one more dangerous

to me than I   who
in my wanting you
have armed you with that knife

O what I would give for a summer ant
now the snow yields only the

hard white berry of the poison ivy
better yet give me a hill

O how I long for their stray punctuation
upon this vacant page

Piscator taught Venator
to angle
under a sycamore tree

you taught me
to gun the gargling engine to
yaw & pitch us free

boat keel up
the spring moon's drunk
the angler

Addressing himself
to the tightrope act
of two pinhead spiders

the dance of three white moths
beside the new green path
one crow's croaking laugh

my three-year-old grandson
reminds me
just how long a short walk can be

Your children claimed
they could see me from
where you lived across the water

they stood on the shore
& waved to a house
on my side of the river

although I never lived there
still they might have seen me
waving goodbye

The smallest tall ship
in the fleet
with the rust-red sails

the littlest wave
at your bare feet
cool fitted for your use

I am *haijin*
& I am *haijin*
abandoned by my muse

N.B. The word "haijin" can mean either haiku poet or cripple.

Heard John Philip Sousa
when I was five
marched around my living room

wholly alive
sixty-four years later
& I'm not being arch

gooseflesh wears me
when I hear the
Stars & Stripes   disaster march

Cricket on a stick
I swing downriver
singing

my idiot song
of summer's gay
sad demise

we love best
those things least
destined to survive

Called a kit or like a cat
a kitten
the newborn rabbit lived

in our garden then
disappeared as if
he had never been

no you would not name him
grew afraid to tame him
foresaw the owl

4'33"

first movement

the wind a kind of animal
                                        legs

second movement

tocsin   against the window   snare of rain

third

                                blood moon
swallowing our shadow

you   uncrossing your legs

My mother marooned
in her last bed claims
she saw a "Jewish bar fight"

last night
she told her nurse
a Black 49ers linebacker

"Ice water   you better
bring me a glass
or I swear I'll kick your ass"

Father safe at last
inside your walls at last
secure from passion's bite

now no word no sun no hinge
of grackle on the wind
can breach your peace

holed up & crib slim
in your thoughtless fortress
you gird yourself in night

Venezuela

The 103rd view of Fuji was
the one no one
had seen

save for Hokusai
who knew we carry
the last views to our graves

found between
the deer & the bucket-ferry
unseeable   but seen

Every man & woman breathes
as I once did

one asleep inside
the other

this ice no thing to calibrate
against another thing

the woman in me thawed in me

we woke   two souls
stitched in   one skin

& she
I would be a screaming
a feedback shriek

you still me still me
strung box on your lap

strum my
depress my
wring dampered chords from my

strings
keys
mouth

why must I be your instrument
who made you God

In snowsleetrain
on the telephone line
the sparrow mounts his mate

wings akimbo tipping
off & on & off &

there's   there's   there's
always something high-wire acrobatic about
lust

some assembly required

I could be the cottontail
who squats
beneath the hosta leaf

you taste so good
who needs a roof
I don't care that I'm all wet

he feasts on the very
green umbrella
that shields him from the rain

As Heraclitus warns us
you & I
two rivers run

& like the Tigris
& Euphrates
we flow into one

civilization is born thus
& is thus
undone

I do like knowing I'm your muse
you wrote
literature will thank me

but   you added   not know me
nor in truth know me
I muse

a cottonwood seed
skirrs down the street
on the wind   on its way   to tree

You caught me
tracked my voice to thicket
my wings as pale as a spring leaf

caught me
locked me
up in glass no gap to answer my escape

dawn you mourned my loss until
a cracked sleigh bell
creaked in your fireplace

I am the flute
with but one gate
the lipless mouth of a dry reed

you are the capful
wind to flow
through the stop   of my throat

O Love which of us truly speaks
which is it   which is it
yellowthroat

Never one for gardening
I plant you still in autumn
dear Tomcat

your heart's stopped seed
I water with my tears
feed with verses from

The Book of Common Prayer

don't worry
nothing I bury
ever comes up

From my inventory of lost things
found in a drawer
one lost night

one hotel matchbook
one pocket watch stopped at
11:41

one pressed petal
one photograph on
one white sheet your stripped silhouette

The maestro threw up his hands
& glowered
at the potted plant

Beethoven on this winter's night
could not keep time
with that

damned cricket with his 5/4 beat
conducting the
Eroica

My clock a bird
to announce each hour
oriole twelve chickadee one

you said you'd be here half past wren
but wren finch & mockingbird
have sung

now robin slurs his syllables
his song the lay
of a maudlin drunk

Twenty years later
my finger remembers
the knife

its simple slip
a milky moon
indexed in my skin

that afternoon
we met to sever
us from our sundered lives

As a housewarming gift
you gave me a sieve
after I lost my home

I should have known then
that you'd never live
with my furious love

you had no room left
in your house to give
shelter to a homeless man

Fifty years after I began this verse
I find the words
to end it

new buds pink my dead apple tree
new green lives
leave their graves in the dirt

how is it you
still love one who
    has put you through cold hell

We bared our breasts to twisters
as they snaked down
mammatus skies

dared God to show His face
or know the reason why

His lightning never answered
but struck the useless ground

missed us
every time

for Michael W. Howard

How could we care
on that bare sand
for famous loves there come to grief

on Plymouth landfall where
we   stripped of history
could wade waist-deep

drift on those forgetful waves
     & you wind your slim white
legs around me

Venezuela
I was eight
when I made my pilgrimage

to the gleaming cross on top
of the city's
seventh hill

a long climb to find out God
is tin graffitied
nailed to wood

El Trigal
Valencia
1960

Babies tractor
the wet sand their
fat knees cutting roads & rivers

& we their doting gods the lovers
of the hum
of their brusque motors

cluck & grin & hover in
their heaven's cramped
oblivion

Flowers' lovers' flesh is paper
rose you tore
petals you pressed

to my lips to harden shards
of parchment in
your keepsake book

my lips once parched
once bruised my lips
you pressed distended petals to

In camera
we who would be three

introduced a witness to
triangulate desire

which photographed us
as we strayed

watched with one
unclouded eye

two lovers who
would be betrayed

by their thoughtless spy

Daily my body
admonishes me
"you are a mortal being"

not that I forget
but the fifty-four-legged
scar down my chest

crawls
like a skinned thing living
on me   a living thing

Dog-eared intercalated
an old volume I
am too thorough spread

spine's dry glue loosing
my pages' hinges
tail & head

& yet I stock my shelves
with orphans no one else
has ever read

When your angel came for you
he sucked the marrow
from your bones

ripped through
your tangled web of nerves
& I   who have no use for God

held you told you trembling you
were blessed
to be thus visited

Mother
I regret that when you implored me to
"bust me out of here"

I did not
though I longed to
wheel you down those sepulchral halls

drive you

to the shore to lie beside you
as you died laughing   on the sand

Time will turn & spill
backwards someday
the checkout counter tabloids say

earth   will be unspun
rise up   our setting sun
uphill   will rivers run

& we'll grow fur then gills then

fall

bassackwards   into   soupy seas

One kiss loosed you
like this thaw
your spate your flood your sudden skin

I know this is wrong
you said   as you bathed me in
your starveling kisses

sooner blame water for its fall than you
your mad rush
to swallow me

At the poetry reading
where I shamelessly read
lines I wrote

for you as you
at the back of the room
stayed weeping

sometimes the pain is worth it
my wise friend on seeing
such beauty said

No gardener has ever died
as far back as
you can remember

so you my rose but for a day
think I will care
for you forever

nothing but a lie your dream
our budding love's
unending summer

La rose de Fontenelle, qui disait que, de mémoire de rose, on n'avait vu mourir un jardinier.
—Denis Diderot

Superman each afternoon
rescued Lois Lane

bullets bouncing
off his chest & yet

she never even knew he was
Clark Kent

& I
was the hapless newsman who

thought that he could rescue you
from you

Love mocked me said I was a fool
to live my safe
& desperate life

seized my hope my home my rule
as I raged through autumn days
like loosestrife

let go my flesh
when my sordid heart had changed
to animal & cage

This painting on my bedroom wall
startles me

the mountain lost in taloned waves
hung here   unseen for years

how long has this   our breaking
been stayed

how long have I   failed to hear
it must be September somewhere

Used to plot my suicide
but then
I do procrastinate

too soon too many friends have died
but then
I am forever late

I guess I should be mortified
I'm past my
expiration date

After I befriended death
I stopped to watch the wind
   swim through the trees

   now my heart breathes
     as the earth breathes

& like Tu Fu
who stood on heaven's edge
   I inhabit my absence

Now that I have ended this book
it is time for me to
rip it up

begin again
for I am undone by what I've done
begin again

I have cupped

fallen birds

in these hands

ABOUT THE AUTHOR

Kenton Wing Robinson takes his middle name from his grandmother's maiden name, as it was she who taught him to read and introduced him to Thomas Carew, her favorite metaphysical poet. Robinson achieved his first notoriety as a poet in the eighth grade, when an English teacher intercepted his poem alleging she had sex with hippopotami. His poems have been published in *AGNI, The Litchfield Review, Connecticut River Review, Rattle, Arsenic Lobster, Lilliput Review, Feminist Studies* and several other journals. He lives in Riverside, Rhode Island.

This book is set in Garamond Premier Pro, which had its genesis in 1988 when type-designer Robert Slimbach visited the Plantin-Moretus Museum in Antwerp, Belgium, to study its collection of Claude Garamond's metal punches and typefaces. During the fifteen hundreds, Garamond – a Parisian punch-cutter – produced a refined array of book types that combined an unprecedented degree of balance and elegance, for centuries standing as the pinnacle of beauty and practicality in type-founding. Slimbach has created a new interpretation based on Garamond's designs and on compatible italics cut by Robert Granjon, Garamond's contemporary.

Copies of this book can be ordered
from all bookstores including Amazon
and directly from the author:
Kenton Wing Robinson
65 Oak Ave.
Riverside, RI 02915.
Please send $25 per book
plus $6.00 shipping
by check payable to
Kenton Wing Robinson

•

For more about the work of Kenton Wing Robinson
visit www.antrimhousebooks.com/authors.html.

www.ingramcontent.com/pod-product-compliance
Lightning Source LLC
Chambersburg PA
CBHW030145100526
44592CB00009B/136